What Am I?

What Kind of REPTILE AM I?

Taylor Farley

TABLE OF CONTENTS

A Crabtree Seedlings Book

What Kind of Reptile Am I?

I have no legs and can smell with my tongue.

What kind of reptile am I?

A snake

I have a big mouth and lots of teeth.

What kind of reptile am I?

An alligator

I have a shell and live in the sea.

What kind of reptile am I?

A sea turtle

I change colors wherever I go.

What kind of reptile am I?

A chameleon

I live in the desert and have a scary name.

What kind of reptile am I?

A Gila monster

Glossary

alligator (AL-i-gay-tuhr): There are two species, or groups, of alligator: the American alligator and the Chinese alligator.

chameleon (kuh-MEE-lee-uhn): A chameleon can catch prey, or the animals it kills to eat, with its super long, lightning-fast tongue.

Gila monster (HEE-luh MON-stur): A Gila monster is a poisonous lizard. It is the largest lizard native to the United States, growing up to 22 inches (56 cm) long.

sea turtle (SEE TUR-tuhl): There are seven species of sea turtle in the world: flatback, green, hawksbill, Kemp's ridley, leatherback, loggerhead, and olive ridley.

snake (SNAYK): A snake cannot chew its prey, it has to swallow it whole.

Index

What Is a Reptile?
A reptile is an animal that has dry, scaly skin. It is cold-blooded, which means its body temperature changes with its environment. Female reptiles lay eggs.

School-to-Home Support for Caregivers and Teachers

This book helps children grow by letting them practice reading. Here are a few guiding questions to help the reader build his or her comprehension skills. Possible answers appear here in red.

Before Reading

- **What do I think this book is about?** I think this book is about different kinds of reptiles. I think this book is about what reptiles like to eat.
- **What do I want to learn about this topic?** I want to learn more about snakes. I want to learn more about why an animal is called a reptile.

During Reading

- **I wonder why...** I wonder why snakes smell with their tongues. I wonder why a chameleon changes colors.
- **What have I learned so far?** I have learned that sea turtles have a shell and live in the sea. I have learned that Gila monsters live in the desert.

After Reading

- **What details did I learn about this topic?** I have learned that a chameleon can catch prey with its very long tongue. I have learned that a snake cannot chew its prey, it has to swallow it whole.
- **Read the book again and look for the glossary words.** I see the word *alligator* on page 8, and the word *chameleon* on page 17. The other glossary words are found on pages 22 and 23.

Library and Archives Canada Cataloguing in Publication

CIP available at Library and Archives Canada

Library of Congress Cataloging-in-Publication Data

CIP available at Library of Congress

Crabtree Publishing Company
www.crabtreebooks.com 1–800–387–7650

Written by: Taylor Farley
Print coordinator: Katherine Berti

Print book version produced jointly with Blue Door Education in 2023 Printed in the U.S.A./072022/CG20220201

PHOTO CREDITS:
snake © Eric Isselee; alligator eye © dangdumrong; alligator © Heiko Kiera; sea turtle © LauraD; chameleon © Baishev; gila monster © reptiles4all; Chameleon page 22 © Svoboda Pavel. All photos from www.Shutterstock.com

Published in the United States
Crabtree Publishing
347 Fifth Ave.
Suite 1402-145
New York, NY 10016

Published in Canada
Crabtree Publishing
616 Welland Ave.
St. Catharines, Ontario
L2M 5V6